Barbara Woodhouse

on

TRAINING YOUR DOG

RINGPRESS

RINGPRESS

Published by Ringpress Books Ltd,
Spirella House, Bridge Road,
Letchworth, Herts, SG6 4ET

Discounts available for bulk orders
Contact the Special Sales Manager at
the above address. Telephone (0462) 674177

First Published 1992
© 1992 MICHAEL CLAYDON WOODHOUSE

ISBN 0 948955 57 0

Printed and bound in Singapore
by Kyodo Printing Co

CONTENTS

FOREWORD

By Patrick Woodhouse

My mother was born in Ireland in 1910 at a boys' public school where her father was headmaster. Both her family and the boys at the school had a great many different animals and thus she grew up surrounded by them from a very early age. Dogs and other animals became so much a part of her life that it was obvious from the start that she would have animals around her all her life.

One of my earliest recollections of my mother was that she was always with one or other of her two dogs. In the early Fifties she had a Great Dane which responded so perfectly to her training that it won numerous prizes for obedience work. She realised that she really did have a gift for training dogs and she decided that she must use this gift to help others train their dogs.

She started professionally in 1951 with a dog training club meeting on Croxley Green, just a few yards from our house, which was called Campions. She soon had a class of 25-30 dogs and their owners every Sunday and this led to the founding of four other training clubs, in nearby towns, which were always full of dog owners wishing to learn. Her weekends and evenings were thus spent doing the thing she enjoyed most, the training of dogs.

Her own Great Danes, Juno and Junia, were trained to such a high standard that they could work in films and on TV programmes by just being shown the action. Then by simply giving them a command or signal, they would act out the part to perfection. Juno, mother's best known Great Dane, became known as " Take 1 Juno" on the sets of the studios where she worked with famous actors like Sir Alec Guinness, Clark Gable, Roger Moore, Eric Morecambe, and many others. Her Great Danes acted in more than eighty TV and movie productions in their careers, and many of the films were produced by my mother and often directed by her as well.

Her career really started to take off when she was invited to do a TV series about dog training for the BBC and the series was to be called: Training Dogs The Woodhouse Way. This series became such a success that it was repeated three times during its first year and led to two more series and a host of appearances on other programmes in which she was interviewed and in which she demonstrated her methods of dog training to TV stars such as Terry Wogan and Michael Parkinson. In the United States the programmes of her dog training became so popular that they are still being shown to this very day. She became known as the "Dog Lady" and her books became some of the best-sellers ever known in America. In 1980 she won the cherished TV award presented by the Pye Corporation as the Female TV Personality Of The Year and went on to win the title of the World's Best Dog Trainer. Since those hectic days she has travelled the world demonstrating her methods to countless dog owners and visiting numerous countries, including the United States of America, Canada, Australia, New Zealand, Singapore and many parts of Europe, before her death in 1988 following a stroke.

I hope that you, the reader, will get a great deal of help from this book and that it will answer all your questions about the difficulties many people experience when training their dogs. I am sure that the sense of achievement you will experience when you have successfully trained your dog to do even the simplest of exercises will give you a sense of oneness with your dog that cannot be bettered by a relationship with any other animal. May I wish you every success with your training and hope that your dog will become, to quote my mother: "A DOG THAT IS A PLEASURE TO ALL AND A NUISANCE TO NO ONE."

Owning a dog is a privilege, says Barbara Woodhouse.

INTRODUCTION

My first aim in writing about dog training is to help the one-dog owner. I feel that the average person who buys a dog, and wants him just to be a friend of the family, has very little idea of how to train the dog so that he gives of his best and is a source of joy, but never of trouble. This object is generally not acquired without some training. Most people expect the dog to fit immediately into their households, although they themselves have not spent any appreciable time on educating him to his new life with them, and they are exasperated when the dog misbehaves. I do not think it is absolutely essential to attend a training course; this is not the one and only way of learning how to train a dog. This is something anyone, man, woman or child, can do in the home, and in my opinion the home is the right place for the training to be carried out. The main use of a training class is that it gets your dog used to other dogs in large numbers, and this teaches him to ignore dogs in the street and not to fight. A further advantage is that the experienced trainer is there at hand to explain how to overcome particular difficulties. I cannot repeat too often that dogs have, in my opinion, a brain equal to that of a child of about five years old. If spoken to as one would speak to a child, and given a chance to understand, the dog will quickly respond to the owner's lasting benefit. You wouldn't turn your five-year-old out in the street to amuse itself, hoping for safety; yet this is expected to work for dogs. I believe that dog owners shape their dogs' characters according to their own, although I have seen some owners with dogs they don't deserve, and vice versa. Dogs have been faithful friends to man for countless ages, and there is no reason why everyone shouldn't own an obedient companion, but in my opinion, it is a privilege to own a dog, a privilege for which one must be ready to make certain sacrifices. We must realise that not everyone likes or tolerates dogs, and that if we are devoted to our dogs, and do not wish to leave them behind when going on holiday, the scope of our holiday is thereby limited. We shall have to choose a hotel or lodging house where dogs are allowed, and what is more important, the dog must be so well trained that complaints about him do not arise; if they do, you are creating a precedent which is unfair to other owners of well-behaved dogs.

Do not listen to people who tell you a big dog cannot thrive in a town or that it is cruel to keep a dog in a flat. A loved dog is happy wherever you live. If he is a loved dog you will see your own living conditions do not deprive him of exercise and a good life. if you have to leave a dog alone in a flat or a house all day, that is no life for a dog, but no real dog-lover would inflict such conditions on his friend. But on the other hand, do not imagine that dogs should never be left alone; a well-trained dog should not require a baby-sitter, but should stay quite happily guarding his owner's property, without barking or whining continuously. Many owners complain that their dogs destroy things if left alone; this is a consequence of bad training, and should be firmly checked. An indoor kennel for a small dog makes destruction impossible in the owner's absence, but a big dog must be trained not to destroy. Again, it is the owner's attitude to these things that matter. If he allows a dog to tear and trample things in his presence, and thinks it funny how can the dog be expected to know that such an activity is wrong when the owner is not there?

One final question. I am always being asked whether a pedigree dog is easier to train than a mongrel. My answer is that all dogs can be trained if the owner is made of the right stuff. If the owner is at fault, you cannot blame or train the dog. As the ancients say wisely:

Have a care o' th' main chance,
And look before ere you leap;
For as you sow, y' are likely to reap

Butler

BARBARA WOODHOUSE

Chapter One

GETTING STARTED

Now I am going to suppose that you have acquired a completely untrained dog of three and a half months or over. The age doesn't matter. Time and time again I am asked, 'Is my dog too old to train at three years or more?' I answer: 'The age of the dog, providing it is not too young, does not matter. I have trained dogs at eight years old, and many times trained them at five and six years old.' Far more important than the age of the dog is the disposition of the owner. I am going to give a few examples of owners I have met, and if you fall into one or another category, I hope you are either duly proud or duly ashamed of yourself.

The first owner arrives usually with a medium-sized or small dog. The dog is shown to me as being quite impossible to train, as probably having been taken to the vet for pills to quieten him down, but all to no effect. I am, I am told, his owner's last hope. The owner is usually a very excitable person, as often as not a woman. Her nervous speech and movements and constant chatter make me realise at once that the dog is only copying his owner when he displays

symptoms of hysteria. He fights other dogs because his owner inevitably gathers him up in her arms or shortens his lead to choking point on approaching another dog, so that the dog at once stiffens and expects a fuss when he sees another dog in the distance. This owner has got to learn that her dog is a good dog if only he is given the chance. I usually take the dog from her and demonstrate that he doesn't attempt to attack other dogs if I take him along with me. I have to make her understand that to train the dog she must believe that she can make him behave, and that it is not witchcraft on my part when the dog behaves with me.

The next type of owner is a very nervous type of man or woman, usually elderly, with a large animal that is far beyond their strength. He or she literally hasn't the physical power to give the dog the sharp jerks on his choke collar that are the preliminary to all good heel work. I tell them I think the dog is too much for them, but they insist that they adore big dogs, and 'he's such a darling' – if only he wouldn't pull them over, steal the joint, go off alone most of the day and chase everything that moves. Again, it is usually me that has to give this dog his first lesson in the meaning of a choke chain collar, in fact I have nearly to choke him before he finally realises that it is far more comfortable to keep to heel on a loose lead than to pull on a collar that tightens round his neck as he pulls.

The next type of owner is the one who arrives with the tiniest toy dog, complete with cushion, and does so want the dog to behave, but he is so tiny to teach anything to. I adore training these mites, and have, in my time, spent many hours on the floor coaxing one of them to retrieve a dumb-bell. I have before now given a sharp slap to a tiny Miniature Dachshund, who with malice aforethought, defied my every command. I have used two fingers only, and been most careful to smack in the right place. Some of these little mites can be extremely stubborn and no amount of coaxing will alter their behaviour. Horror-struck onlookers have wondered how I could do such a thing, but I always maintain that I am the best judge of what to do with a dog. Had the owner been the best judge, it would not have been necessary to attend classes. In every case I punish a dog without feeling angry, and then only after every other means has been tried.

While I am on this matter of smacking dogs, I should like to pass on what I hear from many owners on their methods of punishing their dogs. When the dog is caught in the act of doing something dreadful the owners have several ways of showing their displeasure. Quite often, people tell me 'Oh, I don't speak to my dog all day.'

Can you imagine any dog seeing the point of this? If that is a sensible punishment, then I suppose we are to keep up a constant chatter to our dogs in order that they may understand that we are pleased with them! It sometimes happens that I do not speak much to my dogs in the course of a day; they quite understand, then, that I am very busy or worried. The other night I was both busy and worried, and it wasn't until my husband said: 'Look at your dogs, Missis,' that I glanced at them and saw they were both lying gazing at me, their eyes full of urgent entreaties to go and get their dinner. Both tails were wagging and both heads were lying between their paws. They were relying on their beautiful eyes, that were fixing me with a stare, to make me understand what they wanted, without barking or disturbing my train of thought. Those dogs didn't take my silence as a punishment, but they knew I had temporarily forgotten them. I believe they thought that by concentration and telepathy they would attract my attention: as they would have, before long.

Another type of owner scolds her dog in the most gentle manner possible, being quite certain in her own mind that harsh words may cause severe and permanent injury to her dog. I fear that as a punishment for stealing or biting, or some such deed, this type of mild rebuke will get you nowhere. If your dog is as sensitive as this, one look from your displeased face will send him to the corner in a misery. I believe that if your dog really loves you, and you him, a bond exists between you, so that your merest hint of crossness is conveyed to him without words being said. But I

All breeds of dog can be trained to a high level of obedience, if the owner is prepared to work at it.

maintain that if you have created that bond, you won't be at training classes. The next type of owner gives a sound thrashing for whatever wrong the dog has done, believing the theory that 'the more you beat them the better they be.' This just gets a dog muddled and very unhappy. Some dogs cringe and show every kind of allegiance to this kind of behaviour, and I often think that the animals that do the best heel work, clinging to the sides of their handlers in obedience tests, have had one or two beatings before this level of obedience is attained. I would any day rather see an animal walk quietly to heel in an easy manner than cling in terror to the legs of his owner. But then I do not really approve of the artificial manner of

working dogs in these tests.

To resume: I think experience shows that if by a quick smack you can cut short the nagging necessary to make a dog do something which it is quite imperative he should do, then give a quick smack when you are not in a temper, and immediately show that you bear no malice. Recently it was so cold that instead of having a training class in our Nissen hut I invited the handlers and dogs into my drawing-room and rolled back the carpets. This meant that we had a very confined space, and if we were to gain any benefit from a class under these circumstances, the dogs not working at any given moment must be kept lying down and quiet. This was a good exercise in itself. One young

Poodle would not lie down; he would sit, but while sitting kept up a ceaseless, stupid whimper. I gave the owner instructions as to how to put him down, but the Poodle won every time by getting up again. The dog owner had had every chance to show how the dog should behave, and as the animal was spoiling the class for the rest of the handlers I went over, gave a firm command and the lightest of slaps on his lordship's posterior. He lay down at once, put his head between his paws, and went to sleep. He knew I meant what I said and certainly felt I meant it. When I was ready to have him work I went over to him in a very pleasant manner, and spoke to him amiably; he was delighted to see me, and we had both forgotten the former incident. I need not have slapped him. Had I had time to reason with him I could have made him do exactly what I wanted with nothing but my voice, but in class one hasn't always the time to give the necessary individual attention to each misbehaving dog. I believe the smacking of dogs should not, as a rule, be done by the owners. If the dog is behaving badly enough to require punishment the owner is probably in a temper, and I don't think anyone should hit in a temper. One inevitably regrets it. If a trainer does it in a calm way, without temper, the dog understands what it is all about.

In all future descriptions of how to train your dog I shall leave out all reference to corporal punishment. It is a very distasteful subject to all dog lovers. I have given my views as to the occasions on which it seems reasonable for a dog to be punished in that way,

and I shall always think a dog caught in the act of doing something quite unpardonable is more quickly taught there and then by a sharp slap than by all the talking to in the world. If you need to smack your dog, in my opinion, you have failed, as a trainer, to exert proper influence on him from the beginning. That is why your dog has to be broken of his bad habits the hard way.

Most people come to my courses in the right spirit, realising that to train perhaps twelve dogs and handlers in a total of six and a half hours needs an almost super-human effort on my part; that is, if I am not content just to stand in the middle of a class and yell orders. My idea of training is that all the dogs should learn properly exactly what I set out to teach them, and I am afraid I spend a long time sometimes on a particularly difficult dog, trusting that the other members of my class will forgive the time filched from their own charges. I find this training of dogs the most fascinating work possible. Sometimes it breaks my heart to see the utterly unsuitable owners that intelligent dogs have to put up with. Often I have to train the dog in spite of his owner. Some dogs I know will never be trained after they leave me. Whatever we do in the class is left unpractised directly the class is over. I think some members come for an entertaining weekend, but to those who come and really make progress I always feel extremely grateful. For by the mere fact of having a well-behaved dog on the streets they are helping to spread the gospel that training pays all along the line.

Chapter Two

HEEL WORK

The first exercise must be to train a dog to walk nicely on and off the lead. First you require a choke chain of the required length and type. The thin small links on some that are on the market are quite useless for training a dog kindly. The broader the link the less likelihood of any damage to the dog's coat, and one can get more purchase on the dog with a broad chain than a narrow one. Lengths of these chains vary. Small dogs need sixteen to eighteen inch lengths. Bigger ones, up to twenty-eight inches. Tiny tots need the finer and smaller chains still, although I consider that a very small dog need not have a choke chain at all. Next, you take hold of both rings at each end in different hands, and with one hand held high above the other slowly drop through the lower ring, until both rings meet each other. I once sent a man a choke chain through the post and it came back twice with the remark that he was not a conjuror – the rings wouldn't go through themselves as they were both the same size. The rings do not thread through each other, but the chain is dropped back through one ring.

Now that the chain is correctly threaded, put it on your dog so that the chain pulls in an upward direction when on the dog's neck; in this way the chain immediately loosens when you release the pull on the lead. If you put the chain on so that it pulls downwards when on the dog, it does not free itself but stays tight even though your lead is loose. This means that you are punishing your dog when he should not be punished, and spoils the whole idea of letting your dog realise that as soon as he stops pulling he is quickly comfortable again. This choke chain is in no way cruel; the only effect it has on the dog is he quickly gives up the idea of pulling and becomes a nicely behaved animal.

Now that you have presumably attached your choke chain in the right manner, the correct length of chain should be such that when threaded through itself it has a couple of inches or so loose to spare; that means that it is easily put on over the dog's head. Never try to force on too small a choke chain for this could hurt or frighten the dog. Next, the lead must be fixed to that ring of the chain that is doing the

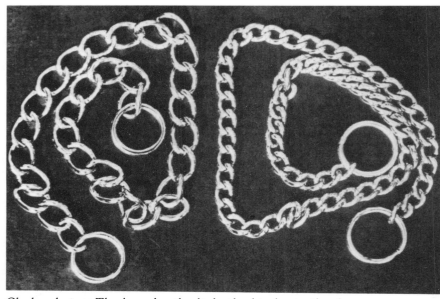

Choke chains: The broader the link, the kinder to the dog.

pulling upwards. The lead must be approximately three to five feet long and of leather. Be sure not to have too wide a leather lead or the edges will cut your hand as you jerk the dog. The lead must have a strong clip, especially for big dogs. I have had little success with the convenient scissor-type of clip. They are inclined to break when you jerk your dog. The Trojan-type clip is the best. (See Appendix for availability of choke chains and leads).

The next step is to get your dog sitting on your left-hand side. Hold your lead in the right hand, over the two middle fingers only, and adjust the length so that when you are walking with your dog, and you are holding your hand slightly across your body, the lead hangs in a loop. It is vitally necessary to have the lead loose when held in the right hand. Now your left hand is free to do any correcting of the dog that is necessary. Should the dog pull on the lead, let him get nearly to the end of the lead and then put your left hand on the lead with your fingers facing the way you are going and your thumbs facing towards yourself, palm downwards; now with a firm command "Heel!" give your dog a very quick jerk back to your side. Take your left hand off the lead immediately; he will be almost certain to forge ahead again, so repeat the quick jerk with the short sharp command "Heel!" prefaced by the dog's name. Always preface any command with the dog's name, to attract its attention. Also try to keep the dog's attention on his work and position by cheerful encouraging word, such as "Good boy, close."

To use: (1) Hold by both rings. (2) Drop chain through one ring. (3) Put on dog pulling upwards. (4) The chain automatically loosens when used correctly.

Correct: The proper way to use a choke chain.

Wrong: A chain incorrectly put on a dog.

Most owners do not jerk their dogs quickly enough, but give a few slow gentle pulls; this is useless, and will never train a dog. Slap your leg to attract the dog's attention, praise him when he comes near to your side, always try the encouraging word before the jerk. Stopping a really bad puller can only be achieved by the most peremptory kind of jerk. It may look rough, but it does not in any way hurt the dog. Most people forget to take their left hands off the lead immediately after the jerk, and therefore spoil the chance of the dog's lead being completely loose after he has been corrected. Always continue walking at a normal pace while jerking. *Never stop to jerk the dog,* or the lesson is spoilt. If the dog drags behind, jerk him

forward in the same manner. If a dog lies on the ground when asked to walk, and no amount of encouraging words will make him stand up and come on, go on walking relentlessly, paying no attention to the dog. In no time he will get up and give up being dragged, and you will have defeated him in the first battle of wills.

I know it is easier to write about these things than to carry them out, but I am not keeping back any of the secrets of dog training just because some people think the procedure heartless. If you wish to take your dog out in the street on a loose lead you may have to achieve what you wish by a clash of wills. I recently dealt with a tiny three-pound Griffon whose owner had had to carry her in her arms for six months as

Heelwork

*(1) The correct
length of lead.*

*(2) Walking
comfortably to
heel.*

(3) Right hand anchors over hip.

(4) Pushing the dog to sit.

she did this lying-down trick. I took her to a carpeted landing and dragged her; in a few seconds, she thought she might do well to mend her ways, and then I took her out for a walk. She has given no trouble ever since. I do not like these battles any more than the owners do, but I feel it my duty to help both owner and dog to live a happier life, and often one short, sharp engagement will do the trick. There is never, in my opinion, any possible excuse for smacking a dog for bad heel work. If you continue to jerk in the right manner you must win. The time it takes depends on the sharpness of your jerks and your skill as a handler. Having got your dog walking better on the lead, you must now teach him to sit every time you stop. This obviates any chance of the dog causing you to be pulled into the road should you suddenly stop on seeing a vehicle coming, for as you stop, however suddenly, your dog sits. Eventually your dog becomes so well trained that he doesn't need the command "Sit" as you stop; he knows what to do. But this high degree of training will not be brought about in a week by the average dog owner without experience.

To get your dog to sit quickly and easily, your lead should be of just the right length, so that as you intend stopping you should place your lead, which is held in the right hand, up and over your right hip. This anchors the dog's head in an upward position and helps you to push him to the 'sit' with the free left hand. This movement is done in 'one-two' time. Up with the right hand on the *one,* and down with the left hand on the *two.* Now the correct position of the left hand should be thus: your four fingers are facing

away from your leg, and should be placed over the dog's back so that the two middle fingers are in his flank just in front of the hind leg. The thumb should now be facing towards your own left leg and should also be placed lightly over the dog's back. On your command "sit", you should, of course, raise your right hand over your right hip and smartly pull the dog down to the 'sit' with the left hand. If you are doing it correctly, the dog cannot do anything but sit. If you are too slow with the left-handed pull, your dog will have got ahead of you and will then be sitting in front of you; this is bad, because you would trip over him as you began to walk again. The secret of a tidy 'sit' beside you is speed; as you stop quickly, pull firmly with the left hand and the right hand goes to your hip. There are, of course, different methods of achieving this 'sit', but I have tried many others and have found the one described infallible for all types of dog and owner. It is just as easily performed by a child as an adult, as the dog is off his balance through having his head raised; and if the actions are done fast enough, he goes to the 'sit' almost before he realises what it is doing. To get a dog to sit well in to your leg, do your practising with a wall on your left side, and walk fairly close to it. This can be done in the street.

We have got our dog to stop pulling or dragging by jerking the lead; we have got him to sit quickly by pushing him down. This is so far, so good, as long as your dog is on the lead, but how do we progress to getting the same results with the dog off the lead? That can only be done when the dog really walks well on lead, and by that I mean that the dog should have left the jerking stage well behind; on the command "Heel", you can count on his being close to your side, and when you about turn or left turn, or right turn, your dog should come with you. The next step is to remove the lead and place your dog on a very light long piece of string, so fine that he will not feel that he has any restraint at all. At first he will try to run away; call him in and if he doesn't come scold him sharply and repeat the command "Heel". He will soon realise that there's no knowing whether he is on the lead or not. And rather than risk a scolding, he will stay to heel. In all the above exercises, and after every exercise, please remember to give unlimited praise to your dog. I always tell my pupils to bring the right hand down and scratch the dog's chest after every exercise. Dogs love this, and stay still with a benign expression on their faces as long as you like to continue it.

The next step is to have no lead or string at all on your dog, and to walk about, calling him to stay to heel. If he does so, praise him at once. It is imperative that you never weary your

dog of this heel work. Never practise it for more than ten minutes at home. In the street, do not allow your dog to pull you about; if he attempts it, correct him firmly. You are quite certain to have a few busybodies accost you and tell you how cruel you are, but their views are of no importance. I expect they think it kinder that the dog should be free to run across the road and kill himself or someone else. We who really love dogs have to put up with a certain amount of ridicule and criticism from stupid so-called dog lovers who cannot bear ever to see a dog corrected. Be comforted, for there are thousands of dogs who hardly need training, they are naturally obedient and well behaved. Their owners are lucky. I, and others like me, are here to deal with the not-so-fortunate owners of adorable but definitely badly behaved dogs. Do not at any time imagine that the training of a dog to absolute perfection is a matter of a weekend's work. It all depends on your dog's temperament, and your ability to absorb and carry out the instruction given to you.

Chapter Three

RECALLS

The next most important task we have to tackle is to get your dog to come when you call him. This lesson is at first taught on a lead. Put your dog on his lead and tell him to stay; walk back to the full extent of his lead, and then call him up to sit in front of you. If he is unwilling to come, a short quick jerk on the lead will pull him to his feet. Encourage him to come to you by putting all the love you can muster into your voice, coupled with a series of quick jerks and the word "Come", prefaced by his name. If he tries to bolt, jerk him sharply with the word "Come", changing to a warm, encouraging voice should he show any sign of coming to you. If you think it will help to give him a titbit on coming, by all means give him one, but drop this habit as soon as is possible or the dog may get disgruntled later on with coming and not getting anything. This recall exercise must be treated as another lesson, not as a meal!

You have now got your dog to come to you on the lead. Sit him in front so that his head touches your knees, or, according to his size, that part of your leg or body he can reach. My Great Dane touches my chest. Then with your lead still in your right hand, give the dog a cheerful command "Heel!" and help him to go round behind you and sit once more on your left-hand side, ready as usual to set off. To get your dog to go round to this position the lead must be passed from the right hand, round the back of you to the left hand, and then back to the right hand, so that you can, as before, push the dog down to the 'sit' with the left hand. If the dog is slow going round behind, you can help him to get there by gently pushing his rump. That means he is being pulled in the right direction with one hand and pushed as an aid with the other hand. I strongly recommend a titbit at first to supplement the reward of your enthusiastic praise when the dog gets to your left side. That left side of you must be the place that the dog comes to associate with love, praise, and the occasional little snack. To get a dog to do this going-to-heel easily, try doing it on a loose lead and flicking the fingers of your right hand as an encour-agement, also patting the left thigh to

Going To Heel On Recall

(1) Dog sits in front of you.

(2) Pass lead to left hand.

(3) Help dog to heel with right hand.

(4) Pass lead over right hip and make dog sit.

Using the cord: Put your dog on a long cord and make him sit.

induce him to come there. The less you pull tightly on the lead, the more easily your dog will learn this act.

Now you are ready to put the dog on a ten-yard cord and make him come in to you in exactly the same way but from a greater distance. Most dogs find it difficult to stay while their owners leave them to get to the end of the cord. Should the dog get up, go back to him and firmly push him to the 'sit' again. Walk backwards facing him all the time, keeping your arm raised and the fingers of the hand extended in a signal that I call the 'abracadabra'. It makes the dog sit very still and take notice, just as if it were under a spell. As you do this, gently repeat the command, accompanied by his name "Stay, Fido" or "Fido, stay", whichever you like best. When you have at last got him to stay,

get to the end of your cord and call him; should he run away, pull him in quickly on your cord and scold him. Then loose him again; at this stage I think he will hesitate, and this is the time to coax and praise him for all you are worth. He thinks this is just the life for him, and usually comes in. Give him a titbit if you want to. If he hesitates and tries to decamp, use his name firmly in a lowered voice, which means (to him) murder if he doesn't obey. At the slightest attempt to come to you, change at once to the loving tone.

I cannot stress too strongly that the tone of your voice is the secret of efficient training. Some people literally cannot alter their voices enough to make their dogs listen to them and perceive a change of mood. Such folk can register neither love nor

The Command: Gently, but firmly, pull the dog towards you.

displeasure. This is a great disadvantage in dog training and makes the handler's task a difficult one. I often say I would like my pupils to leave their dogs at home and come for a voice training lesson before attempting to teach their dogs. People have often asked why their dogs behave well with me and not with them, and I have explained that my tone range makes me sound exciting to the dog, or cross, or adoring, and in each case the dog responds accordingly. I have often demonstrated this by using the most hateful words to a dog in a loving voice, and the tail has wagged in the happiest manner. Alternatively I have said the most loving things in a stern voice, and the dog has cringed and been miserable. In dog training it is how you say things, not what you say, that matters.

Your final object is to make the dog come instantly on command; not, as I have said elsewhere, when he feels he might as well come since there is no more attractive prospect; not simply because he is tired of what he is doing. We now assume you have got your dog to come on the cord at all times. Next you must get him in an enclosed space and practise with the same tone of voice and commands with him off the lead. A landing is a good place for practice, or an enclosed yard. If he does it well, always take him for a walk in an open space. Practise on the cord first of all, and then without the cord. If the dog runs away go back to the cord and practise further. This business of making a dog come when he is called has two aspects. If the dog imagines he is going to get scolded when he does come, he naturally sees no point in coming. So many people, having chased their dogs for ages, at last capture the animals and proceed to beat them. That is fatal. If the dog comes to you, even after an hour, by himself, he must be praised, however evil you feel. If, however, you actually catch the dog as he is bolting away, then you must reprimand him.

Most dogs adore being chased and, seeing a pursuer, run all the faster. A great many fall into the trap of hastily following you if, instead of chasing them, you turn round and run in the opposite direction. The dog races after you and a sudden turn round on your part makes a capture possible. I feel very strongly that any dog that runs away from his owner is not attached by that loving bond that should exist between owner and dog. I feel that this dog is one that has been turned or let out in the garden to amuse himself. This sort of treatment is not kindness, but is pure laziness on the part of the owner. The dog's place at all times should be with his owner; left to his own devices he gets into mischief and develops an independent set of habits through being forced to be by himself. I cannot believe that any dog that has the advantage of constantly being with its owner would enjoy running off. He has become used to being a constant friend and companion. We know many people who keep dogs say they are too busy to exercise them, and just turn them out, but I have proved that dogs need very little exercise. It is exercise even if they are merely following some member of the household from room to room as

she goes about the usual household tasks. Many dog owners see their dogs for only a short period each day. They are too busy to do otherwise. Are we, in spite of such a drawback, to deny these people the companionship of a dog when they come home in the evening? I think not, but I do think they cannot, on such terms, expect the dog to obey them instantly when so little of their lives is shared with the dog. It is particularly these people who should spend time in the evenings practising the art of training and getting to know their dogs better.

Some dogs have the natural hunting instinct deeply ingrained and it is these dogs that are the most dangerous to domestic livestock, and the least to be relied upon without training, to return to the owner on command. Such dogs should be given a great deal of work of some kind to divert these natural instincts. A dog that does advanced obedience training, and receives much deserved praise, gets this joy and energy expenditure in such work, but other dogs just get into mischief. The trouble is that owners buy the wrong sort of dog for their circumstances. I expect a good many owners will be annoyed or distressed to read that I believe their dogs do not really love them enough if they prefer freedom to the owner's company; but they might reflect that our public houses are filled on most evenings with somewhat similar human beings, who prefer the company of acquaintances to that of their wives. Dogs can be 'almost human' !

Chapter Four

THE STAY

By now, having got your dog to walk to heel on and off the lead, you can progress to one of the most difficult of exercises, that of teaching your dog to stay at the 'sit' or the 'down' when you go out of sight. This is essential with a town dog who likes to accompany his mistress shopping. Many shops nowadays, regardless of licked fingers and of hands unwashed after nose-blowing and so forth, not to mention ash-dropping customers, pin up notices requesting that 'in the interests of health, will customers not bring their dogs into the shop'. So far as untrained dogs are concerned, I agree whole-heartedly. Some dog owners are indescribably lax in allowing their dogs to lift their legs and soil over shop doors, and even over vegetables in shops. It is thanks to this sort of owner that decent, right-minded owners must also keep their dogs outside. As this exclusion is now general in many districts we should all endeavour to train our dogs so that they can accompany us so far, and yet comply with the shopkeeper's request. It is quite easy to train your dog to sit or lie down outside a shop; harder to train

are the general public who cannot leave your dog in peace. It takes years of training to get a dog to that state where it will stay put under the most trying circumstances. In my classes I attempt to emulate the public. I bend down and stroke the dogs, I drop my handbag near them, I climb over them, I walk other dogs all round them, and generally do my best to upset them. But the trouble is that as they know me, the test is not strict enough. If it were possible to practise with strangers, the lesson would have more value.

Here is the way to begin training your dog to wait outside for you. If you had him as a puppy, you would already, we hope, have carried out the instructions for making him stay alone in another room, but I am going to presume you have only just acquired an adult dog, and are about to train him to wait. Get out the familiar cord, so useful in dog training. Put your dog on to it, and as he has already learnt to 'stay' while you go to the end of the cord (in the recall) repeat this as the beginning of the exercise. Then return to him while he is still on the cord and immediately leave

Hand signals are all-important. This 'abracadabra' signal ensures the dog stays put, giving you all his concentration.

him again, at first giving him the command "Stay!" as you leave. Should he get up, push him down again, and leave him again. Get him thoroughly used to this, and then if you have a garden put him to 'sit' or 'down' in the garden and walk into the house. Watch him, and the moment he moves, shout "Down!" from your window without letting him see you. He will not know where the voice is coming from, but will probably drop again, comforted by the fact that you are about. Every time he moves repeat the command, then return to him, keeping him 'down' until you are right up to him, and then let

him up and praise him for all you are worth. Never leave a dog at the 'sit' for more than two minutes: it is a tiring performance. If you intend leaving the dog for longer than that, put him to the 'down'. This is easier to write than to accomplish. I am always surprised at the number of dogs who strenuously resist being made to lie down. Why, I can't imagine, for it is a natural and restful position. There are at least three ways of putting a dog 'down'. The first is a simple if rather slow method, and a good one to start on. The second is a quicker but more difficult method, mostly used by those having to deal with very strong dogs. I use the command 'down', for I detest the word 'flat': it is a hard, uncomfortable word. 'Down' can be a caress and an assurance all in one, and if ever a dog needs assurance it is when a loved owner leaves him alone. I have seen owners in murderous temper with their dogs in the show ring obedience tests when the dog has got up when supposed to be lying down, but I believe that this happens because the dog has not trusted his owner enough. He is frightened lest maybe the owner should not come back. Do not we human beings feel worried enough to go a hundred times to the door when a loved one is late coming home? Such anxiety is quite understandable. Yet a dog must not have any such fears, and if he dares to get up and look around him, he is punished. I know he must learn this exercise for his safety's sake, but I wish owners would give more comforting words to their dogs as they leave them. I see owners leaving their dogs without a smile or a backward glance, and uttering the most aloof "Stay", yet they expect the dog to be happy while awaiting their return. Leave your dog with a pat and a kind word, give it a very slow firm command, "Stay". Don't leave him and go out of sight until he will stay for a long time when you are still in sight; then slowly go farther and farther away. Should the dog get up when you are still in sight, then is the time to be firm and rather cross. He has no excuse for anxiety when he can see you, and is showing disobedience that must be firmly checked. No soft: 'Do lie down for Mummy's sake' is any good in this case; a firm command and push down are indicated.

To get a dog to lie down without frightening or hurting himself or you in any way, put him at the 'sit', then lift one foreleg with one hand and gently push the opposite shoulder towards the leg you are raising. This puts the dog off his balance and he has to go down. As soon as he is down, scratch his chest and praise him. The second way to make a dog lie down, if he is walking on your left side, is to grasp the running end of the choke chain in the right hand, still holding the lead, turn the hand until the palm faces ahead of the dog's nose, stand facing your dog's side with legs wide apart for balance; in this position, place your hand on the ground a few inches ahead of the dog and with the other hand press on his back. The pressure on the choke chain forces the dog's head down and the back pressure helps to overbalance him. Usually it only takes a minute or two to teach a dog this, if you use a firm command "down" at the same time exerting the pressure on collar and back. I definitely prefer the first shoulder-pushing method for beginners, but the other method is quick and easy if you do it with lightning speed, and of course, it does get your dog lying down directly beside you in a crouching position, whereas the shoulder-pushing method gets the dog down in a 'curled over' position. This latter position, incidentally, is quite essential if you intend leaving a dog for a long time. A crouching dog can get up quickly, but a dog in the 'curled' position has first to get into the crouching position before he can rise. If you use the lead method of dropping your dog, gradually get the lead longer and less tight. I find that after I have done this about six times, a dog will

Putting a dog in the 'down'

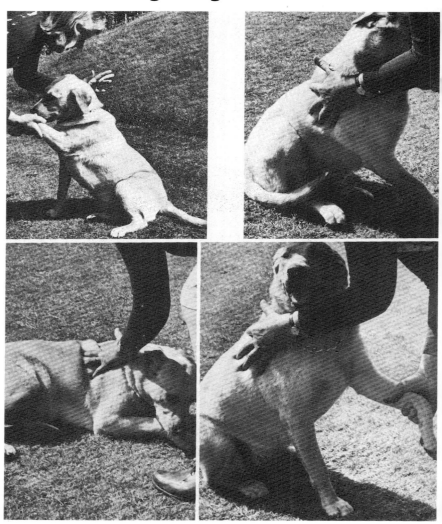

(1) Lift front leg and push opposite shoulder. (2) Push quickly with left hand. (3) Dog lies down. (4) Correct position on dog's shoulder.

The 'down'

(1) Place left foot on running end of choke chain, keeping right hand held high. (2) Assert pressure with left foot. (3) Release pressure on choke chain as soon as dog is down.

drop on my placing my hand on the ground in front of him, anticipating the tug on his collar which he finds unpleasant. The third method is to stand beside your dog raising the right hand holding the lead, and placing the left foot over the running end of the choke chain quickly pulling the dog to the ground.

In teaching your dog to stay outside shops it is essential to get the help of friends who will accustom the dog to having strangers walk near him, and perhaps bend down and touch him. That is one of the great advantages of a training class. So many people are rushing back to their dogs, or yelling at them, or falling over them, that the dogs get used to the most fantastic noise and disturbances. I have noticed in classes that no one thinks of the possibility of anyone else's dog getting upset by his sudden rush to reprimand his own dog. This, of course, certainly helps to train the other handlers' dogs, for there is no chance here for a nervous dog to show temperament. The extraordinary thing is that I have constantly found the most nervous dogs forgetting their nerves in this melee and becoming quite used to strangers jumping over them. Biting dogs no longer bite passers by; in fact, the relentless bustle and constant motion and uproar seem to help a nervous dog, rather than make him worse. As I have said before, a good deal of patience will be required before you will be able safely to leave your dog outside a shop. You need to practise by leaving the dog with his lead still attached at first, and keeping a watchful eye on him all the time. But with practice he will learn to ignore all passers-by.

In this book I have often used the words 'scold' or 'get cross with' your dog; this may mean just switching to a sad tone of voice while using his name, or even putting on a shocked look, or addressing him with a flood of cross words, or giving him a shaking. It all depends on the nature of the bond between you and your dog. If you are an owner who only talks to his dog when the rare mood takes you, you will probably have to use far harsher methods than someone who has a dog that is spoken to at every hour of the day and really understands change of tone and even expression. If I say "Junia" in a sad voice and don't smile when I say it, my dog is sufficiently punished and slinks off in shame; but then she really understands my words and moods; we share our lives completely; she worries with me, she rejoices with me, and if she does wrong, she knows without my scolding that I am annoyed. Only a forgiving word will make her happy again, and I never prolong my disapproval for more than a minute or two, as she would be sick with sorrow if I did.

Chapter Five

DISTANT CONTROL

I teach the handlers in my class distant control in a long line with their dogs at the end of the lead facing them. But it can be done alone at home just as easily. I give the command "Now" and the handlers give their dogs the same command as my next. Should I say "Down", the handlers must raise their right hands and bring them sharply to the ground with the command "Down"; the dogs must instantly drop to this position. They should do this without fuss if they have been trained step by step from this book. My next command may be "Sit". The owners must repeat it to their dogs, and in doing so give the command by voice and the signal by raising their right hands from the ground to above the head. The command "Sit" should be given in a short quick word, not drawn-out like the command "Down". Change of tone of voice (I cannot say this too often) matters enormously in these exercises. If the dog does not go quickly to the 'sit', help him up by lifting him on the lead which should have been under his chin anyway, or by touching his front foot nails lightly with your foot so that

he naturally breaks away into the 'sit'.

Next I shall give the command "Stand". The owner repeats the command and the signal is a slap on the thigh of one leg, which encourages the dog to begin to come to you. As soon as the dog is standing, check him coming towards you with the command "Stay", which of course he should now know. Should the dog not stand, run your hand between his front legs along his chest to his tummy, and lift him up on to his back legs. Alternatively, lift him up with both hands placed just inside his back legs at the thigh and stand him firmly on his legs. As your dog improves on the lead, put him on the cord and do the whole thing at a greater distance. He will at first try to advance towards you; this must be checked with the command "Stay", after the ordinary command. Even in competition work the dog is allowed six feet to move forward, so don't worry too much at first if he can't stick to this; it is a goal to work for. If he came too far forward in the street he would get run over. I should teach a small dog on a table, a large one at the top of the

Advanced work

ABOVE: Leave the dog at 'stand'.

LEFT: 'Sit'.

ABOVE: 'Down'

LEFT: End the exercise with the dog at the 'sit'.

Distant Control

1. Drop the hand and give the command 'down'.
2. Raise hand and give the command 'sit'.

3. *Give the command for the dog to 'stand'.*
4. *Slap your leg for emphasis.*

stairs, so that they can't come forward. Eventually, when the dog does the exercise well, remove the cord and do it again with the dog free. We do six successive commands. Never repeat this exercise ad nauseam, for it is very tiring for the dog and requires great concentration on the part of the owner and dog. Once the dog has learnt it well, abandon it except for an occasional reminder. I hope you will never need to make much use of it.

Having accomplished the teaching of distant control, you want to practise it by leaving your dog at a distance, calling him, and when he's running quickly towards you, giving him the signal and command "Down". If you have trained him properly he should drop instantly and wait for you to call him up when all is safe. In Obedience Trials this is called 'Drop on Recall'; it may be done there either by word or signal, but not both. I strongly disagree with this. I fail to see that in an emergency an owner wouldn't use a command and signal if the dog's or somebody's life depended on it, but then I am an outlaw where these fantastic rules are concerned. I love to see a dog working, but I like it only when it is a joint effort of understanding and brains on the part of both dog and owner. These silent masters and mistresses in the obedience ring can keep their dogs that way if they wish, but I defy anyone to say that the dog likes it. I believe that those dogs, bouncing about as if they were happy, are really a mass of nerves wondering whether they have done right. I am not a 'sour grapes'; my former dog won sixty-seven of these tests, but she and I hated every one of them. It was only that in order to be able to train other people and dogs, one had to prove that one could train one's own dog first. This is the only reason I took part in these tests.

Some people think it is cruel to teach a dog tricks. My dog does endless tricks; and how she loves doing things for me! She arches her neck in pride when she has done something particularly clever, and wants to hear me say so. I love praise if I have done something well; so do children, and so do animals. If I am working her in a film she can't wait until after the Director has said "Cut" to dash round to everyone in the studio to hear how clever she has been. I can teach my dog anything new in a few minutes, and providing I can talk to her and praise her immediately after doing it, she adores it. Opinion is divided about teaching dogs tricks. Is it cruel, people ask? I fail to see that cruelty comes into it unless the tricks taught are for a circus or some such affair when the dog has to perform at a fixed time however little he may feel like doing so. Most dogs love the household tricks we all know, asking for food by begging or barking, playing hide and seek, trusting, etc. I think they join in the family spirit which encourages this harmless fun. A dog already trained in simple obedience is so very easily taught tricks, and I think likes 'being clever'. If he does not enjoy them, then I think it is cruel to force him to become a performer.

Chapter Six

RETRIEVES

Training a dog to retrieve and seek back is another exercise which I think most dog owners should teach their dogs. Its practical advantage is that if you happen to be out walking and drop something, your dog will go back and look for it and retrieve it. Most of the dogs who come to my class and are given a dumb-bell for the first time, rush after it and joyfully pick it up. Some even bring it back to their owners. But it is these eager dogs who are the first to get tired of doing it, and who have to start all over again later. So we are going to teach our dogs the right way from the beginning and ignore their natural desire to retrieve, which may soon peter out if not properly directed.

First of all we use a dumb-bell, because it has big ends to make the centre bar stand up off the ground; this enables the dog to pick it up easily. The dog must never be allowed to pick it up by the ends or chew it. I keep my own high up on a shelf, and as I give it to my dog I use an excited tone of voice as if it were the greatest treat to be allowed to retrieve dumb-bells! Now we begin with the dog on the lead at the 'sit'. Gently open the dog's mouth by inserting your finger into the side of the mouth where there are no teeth, immediately behind the large canine tooth, always keeping your hand on top of the dog's nose, not trying to pull down the bottom jaw. When the mouth is open pop the dumb-bell in with the other hand. *Don't push it back into the dog's mouth,* just balance it behind the canine teeth and allow the dog to close his mouth on it. If you shove it roughly into the mouth you will frighten and hurt the dog, and your task will become more difficult. Should the dog try to spit it out, as most of them do, put it firmly back with the command: 'Hold'; to help him do this, scratch his chest with the other hand, for dogs will hold dumb-bells for a long time so long as this pleasant scratching continues. Their docility enables you to say: 'Give' in a kind voice and take the dumb-bell away. Always take it out of the dog's mouth with two hands, holding the ends, never with one hand only. Repeat this, making the dog hold the object until he does so quite happily. I often advocate a titbit after he has held it well.

Retrieving the dumb-bell

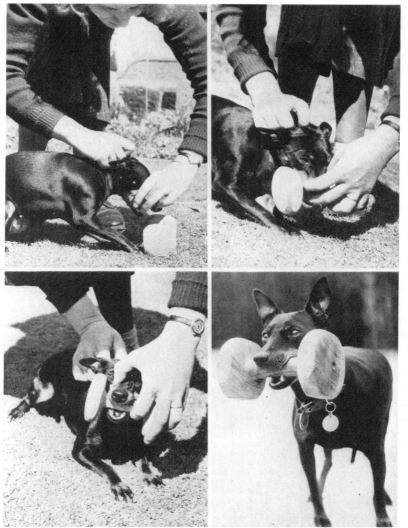

(1) Place finger in dog's mouth and push head down. (2) Push dumb-bell into mouth with second finger. (3) Allow dog to close its mouth. (4) He's got it!

The next step is to make him walk holding the dumb-bell. If you can get him to stay holding it when he is at the end of your long cord, and then make him bring it to you, you have surmounted a real difficulty. But if not, just be satisfied for the time being with getting him to walk beside you holding it, tell him to sit, still holding it, and then taking it away with the "Give" command. Praise him ardently if he has done it well. Some dogs are unbelievably stubborn over this exercise, and will not hold the dumb-bell. They spit it out and fight to avoid holding it. But dozens of times I have made a dog hold a dumb-bell when the owner has failed, and this is done only by showing the dog that your will is every bit as strong as his, and that if necessary you will go on until midnight if he means to defer holding it that long. In the end I always win, but that is more than I can say for many handlers with weaker wills and less determination than I have. Patience, firmness and love are the essentials.

We will presume you are a good handler and that your dog now holds the dumb-bell as soon as it is given to him. Next, you have to teach him to pick it up. This is done by standing beside your dog, with one hand holding the dog's scruff, or loose skin on the neck, while gently pushing his head down until his mouth is over the dumb-bell. Then, with the other hand, you open his mouth by inserting the first finger into the side of the mouth, and pop the dumb-bell into his mouth with the second finger. Let him close his mouth and tell him to "hold". Eventually your dog opens his own mouth as you push his head down, and later on, with

infinite care and encouragement and practice, your dog will pick it up himself. Once he has accomplished this, give the command "Hold" and run backwards; the dog will follow you, holding the dumb-bell. Turn round sharply and tell him to sit; push him down if he doesn't do it quickly enough, still telling him to "Hold". Then take the dumb-bell with the word "Give" and send your dog behind you to your usual left-hand side. Now you are getting on.

There is one enormous fence still to get over, and that is the sending of your dog to fetch the dumb-bell. The best way I know is for you to get a friend to help. Ask your friend to hold on to the long cord which you have put your dog on; you must then make the dog sit by your side, throw your dumb-bell, and encourage the dog to go after it. If the dog won't do so, get your friend to pull the dog towards the dumb-bell on the cord. The dog should now, receiving much praise, pick up the dumb-bell and return to you, sitting in front holding it quietly until you take it, after which you will send the dog to heel on your left side. It doesn't usually take long for the dog to understand this 'going' part of the exercise. Lastly, you must teach him not to go after the dumb-bell: that he must not chase moving things without command. If this precaution is neglected, one day the children may be playing ball with the dog in the garden, and the ball may roll out into the road; and then, if the dog is untrained, it would rush after it. A trained dog waits for the command to get it. I usually recommend owners to hold their dogs by their collars and give the command "Wait" until the dog understands what is wanted of him, and will sit quietly after

Scent discrimination: The dog must learn to pick up objects carrying his owner's scent.

the dumb-bell has been thrown until given the command "Fetch".

Before we can go any further with the 'seek-back' exercise, which consists of making your dog retrace your steps and find what you have dropped, you must teach him only to pick up your article carrying your scent; otherwise he may bring someone else's property, not yours. This exercise is called 'scent discrimination' in official circles, so I

shall use this name. Most dogs enjoy this. The best way to teach a dog this exercise is once more to enlist other people to put articles on the floor, or on the grass. Use such things as purses, clothes-pegs, match boxes, gloves, handkerchiefs, in fact anything the dog might come in contact with in everyday life. Next you decide what you wish the dog to find, let's say your glove. Place the glove, for a minute or two prior to doing the exercise, under your armpit; the dog will then pick up a good scent of you. Next, without letting the dog see it, place it among the other articles, not too closely jumbled at first. Then take the dog on his lead up to the articles, pointing to each one as you walk by it, saying, with some excitement "Seek", good boy, seek". Use a most inspiring tone, as though rats were his quarry. Usually when the dog reaches his owner's article he grabs it, and then you should praise him immediately; but should he pass it by, return to it, and show it to him, pick it up and use it to play with him. Then take him away, get it put down for you again, and try once more. This time he is almost certain to find the right article, so praise him and have a game with it.

Continue like this, with different articles all the time, until he knows that he must only find the one carrying your scent. Should he attempt to pick up the wrong article, say "No" crossly, take it away, and show him the right one. As soon as your dog has learnt thus to pick out your particular article only, teach him to bring it back to you as with the dumb-bell; and, as before, 'sit' in front

and go round to heel to finish with. Now that we have taught the dog to find and retrieve any article, we are ready to teach him the 'seek back'. Go for a walk, and on your way drop something on the path that shows up well – for instance, a handkerchief. Walk on about twenty yards and in a very excited tone of voice tell the dog to 'seek back', pointing to where you have come from. The dog probably won't understand, so run back, encouraging him to go away and seek all the time. Nine times out of ten he sees the handkerchief and picks it up. Then you must praise him with extravagant enthusiasm. Make him do this quite often on your walk; he will soon understand and enjoy the game. As he gets better at it, hide the article in grass near where you have been. That will teach him to cast round and look. Make it more difficult as the dog gets to understand, and you will soon have taught your dog something that may be very useful. One of my friends recently lost her house keys in a wood. She had trained her dog, and he went back over her tracks and found them. Needless to say, she was delighted.

Chapter Seven

ADVANCED TRAINING

The uses of the 'send away' exercise, in my opinion, are few. Perhaps it teaches your dog to go straight home should he insist on following you when you leave home and want him to stay behind. In Test C at shows the dog must go on a single command or signal in a dead straight line and continue going until you are told to drop him down. He must drop to the ground and stay there with you walking past him until you call him up. Marks are lost for a deviation from a straight line, no extra commands are allowed to change the dog's direction should he be going crooked, or you lose marks. This seems to me a pointless exercise. But as some of my readers enjoy competitions, I shall do my best to teach the necessary handling for this lesson.

I teach this on the long cord again, if the dog shows no signs of leaving you when you say "Away" or "Go". Our dog has already learnt to go and fetch the dumb-bell, leaving you in order to do so, so it shouldn't be too difficult to go a step further and make them go and 'fetch' nothing. Let us assume that the dog will not budge at all. The trainer or helper must take the cord, as usual, some distance away from the dog. The dog is sitting quietly on the left-hand side of the owner and is given the command "Away" with the right arm pointing in the direction he is supposed to go; if he does not move, help him by repeating the command and giving him a simultaneous shove in the right direction. Keep repeating "Away", and stamp your foot as if you were going to chase him. He doesn't understand. Very well, ask your friend to pull him on in the cord, while you keep pointing and saying "Away".

When he has gone a little distance, give him the command "Down". He should know this, and drop; walk up to him, telling him to stay, walk round him and away, and then call him to heel. Praise him. Sometimes one can short-cut this method by another one. This is to put your dog at the 'sit', tell him to stay, and walk away some distance where he can see what you are doing, bend down and rub your hand vigorously on the ground, come back to your dog, and give him the "Away" command. Very often he will rush off to see what you did; you can then drop him and the exercise is begun. I find the other method better. This 'Away' exercise takes a long time to teach and reach perfection.

Waiting on command is an advanced exercise used in Test C in competition work, when it is called: 'Advance Stand, Sit, and Down'. Here we are going to study it in relation to its usefulness to the ordinary dog owner. The idea is to make your dog stop instantly on command when you are in motion, either at the 'stand', 'sit' or 'down', so that you can run or walk on without him, and without worrying about his behaviour. There may come an emergency in your life when this exercise might save someone's life. You might, for example, see a small child toddle into the street in the path of a car; with the command "Wait" your dog would instantly stand still, and unhampered you could rescue the child from its peril. On the other hand, you might just want to leave your dog in the drive for a second and run back to get something from the house without his coming; on the command: 'Wait' he would stay where he was until your return.

We teach this exercise in class by having helpers who walk behind the handler and dog, and on the trainer's command "Now" the handler drops the lead near the helper, who places a foot on it, and with a firm command "Wait", the dog is left in the standing position until the handler has made a circle and returned to the dog. He picks up the lead, and with the command "Heel" and a word of praise continues walking. On the next command "Now" from the trainer, the handler repeats the exercise with the dog this time put quickly to the 'Sit'. And so it is repeated, at the third time the dog being put to the 'down'. The idea is to teach your dog to stop instantly and to expect the owner back in a reasonably short time. It is quite amazing how quickly dogs learn this exercise. I find the 'stand' is the most difficult to teach them as they have learnt before this to sit at all times when not walking. If your dog sits when you wish him to stand, run your left hand quickly under his tummy and lift him to the 'stand' with a further command "Wait!" He won't mind this, and it soon teaches him. Don't forget to give the command "Wait" in a quick tone not a long drawn-out voice. Emphasise the 't' in the word 'Sit' and the 'D' in the command 'Down'.

When your dog has got used to being left with the helper, who must in no way touch your dog (he is only acting as an anchor), the next step is to leave your dog without a helper, but with the lead still on. You must practise alone in a room or your garden until the dog never moves until you come back. Next of course, you must take the lead off and repeat the exercise again. Practise it at a walking pace and then at a run. At the end of the three exercises give your dog a vast amount of praise. I use cheerful words in the middle of the exercise, like "good boy" (or "girl") so that the dog will realise he has not finished after one part of the exercise. But at the end of the three commands well carried out I bubble over with joy and praise!

Chapter Eight

GUARDING

A dog's reaction to greeting strangers leads to the more serious aspect of how to teach a dog to guard the home and person of his owner. We must of course divide this question into two parts: the behaviour of puppies, and that of adult dogs. Dealing first of all with puppies, I would much rather see and meet an over-friendly puppy than one that slinks away shivering and shaking when strangers come to the house, for it is the shivery and shaky ones that may eventually be the cowardly biters of the future. How does the mind of a dog work in this matter of protecting the household he belongs to and their property? I believe under the age of twelve months old he hardly reasons it out at all. People who ring me up and tell me their five-month-old puppy is useless for guarding their house need to understand that, if a puppy barked and guarded at that age, in all probability he would be savage and a pest when adult. The development of the mind in different breeds of dogs varies vastly. A St Bernard might not be fully developed at two years old, while a Terrier may behave like a grown dog at twelve

months. One cannot compare breeds or an individual dog's development as regards their protective instinct, or their desire to be a guard dog.

The upbringing of a dog counts for so much in these matters. Most puppies of up to, say, six months or over are boisterous and friendly to all, unless they have nervous temperaments, and that is how it should be. If they are put out into the garden for long periods to find their own amusement they will probably become scatty, and bark at everyone for a long time. The reason for this is that the early developing mind of a dog doesn't know who or what to guard. But when kept in the house with his owner the place to be guarded is quite plainly defined in the dog's brain. The garden however is a very different matter, especially in a built-up area with lots of people passing by.

At first the dog is quite good, he only barks at people who enter the premises, then he finds to his delight that they pause when he barks, and he begins to feel superior and important; thus his lack of respect towards mankind commences. Next he tries barking at people walking down the road, and passing dogs, cars, bicycles, etc; perhaps even starts running up and down the fence with his hackles up, showing all and sundry what a brave dog he is. He gets bolder and, as a tradesman enters the gate carrying something, he goes up to him barking. The tradesman automatically raises in the air whatever he is carrying to get it out of the way of the dog, and the dog interprets that as a sign of weakness, his ego grows, his fierceness increases, and now people who enter the gate find quite a nasty dog barking at them, who refuses to go to the owner who is calling him or to stop barking when told. They back out of the gate and shut it in his face. That act alone annoys the dog and the result is, he bites the next tradesman who comes in. That is how a nasty-tempered dog takes his first bite at a human being.

In the dog's mind he is not only keeping strangers away from his home, but he is showing his superiority over man. Unless he can quickly be broken of this habit he will get worse. The owner is powerless to make him stop barking because he has probably not been trained to come when called, and therefore he wins all round. If, however, a dog is systematically trained to give warning of the approach of everyone to the house by barking when kept in the house, the owner can easily make him stop doing so by making him lie down with the command "Cease" followed by "down". If he doesn't stop, a sharp jerk on the choke chain will do the trick. The dog recognises authority, and quickly learns that to bark in the first place receives praise, but not to stop barking when told earns him a

reprimand. As with so many matters connected with dog training, it is essential to start as you mean to go on. If you want your dog to act as a guard, I believe the correct attitude to take is this: when the bell rings at the front door the householder with a young dog should put on his most excited tone of voice and rush to the door saying "Who is it? See 'em off!" so that the dog barks in excitement. Next, as you approach the door to open it, give the command "Wait". If you have trained your dog my way he will know that this means: 'Stand and stay standing where you are.' To teach this, put the dog on his lead attached to the end of which should be a seven-pound kitchen scales weight, and suddenly, when walking, give the command "Wait" and at the same time drop the lead to the ground. The dog quickly gets used to being checked by word and weight, and soon learns what he must do to get the praise he waits for when he's done right. Now this lesson comes in useful, for he will not go further to greet the strangers or friends until released with the words "Good boy", or "girl" as the case may be. If your friends are dog lovers your dog will probably come in for some friendly pats as he obediently stands there, and you will get the reputation of owning a well-trained dog. If this exercise presents difficulty to you, you haven't practised enough; if the dog drags the seven-pound weight after your leaving him at the stand, use the fourteen-pound one. Never allow a dog to defeat you in anything you wish to do.

Your dog must as far as possible always be with you in all you do; you must be indispensable to him. That is why two dogs together in one household are never so easy to train; they do not depend on their owner for everything, and may not care whether the owner comes or goes. These are the dogs most likely to greet everyone as friends as they have no real allegiance to anyone. How, from a dog's point of view, is he to know who are your friends and who are unwanted intruders? Some dogs undoubtedly seem to sense this by instinct. Most judge people by their scent, and we suspect that fear in humans produces a strong scent perceptible to dogs. Therefore I think we can conclude that an intruder facing a dog feels fear and sends out this scent, but some people do not like dogs and also send out this scent, although they are welcome on the premises. And so it seems sensible to me to train dogs to give warning barks at the approach of foe and friend and to stop doing so when told. Burglars have been known to be great dog lovers and have been welcomed by guard dogs, so I think it is difficult for a dog to know a burglar all by himself. Having trained your dog to bark, he should clearly understand his duty and beyond that we needn't go. Special guard dogs must receive specialised training for their work, and that training is not for the ordinary owner to teach. It is a very personal and rigid training only to be undertaken by experts for experienced handlers to work the dogs, never for the ordinary householder, for a guard dog is potentially dangerous, and ordinary people couldn't manage them, and don't live under suitable conditions to keep one.

Some time back I got a letter from a farmer who complained that he had four or five German Shepherds to guard his poultry farm and that they wouldn't guard, that they were unreliable with his wife, and didn't seem to care twopence whether he or his family existed or not. 'Yet,' he complained, 'I have one in my office on its lead when I am there.' He wanted to know how to train them to guard and, if necessary, attack intruders. I think he expected me to write back with detailed instructions out of the *Police Manual On Dog Training*, if there is such a book, but instead I asked him what affection he gave those dogs. Did he ever take them for lovely walks, or play with a ball with them? Why, I asked him, was the one in his office tied up on a lead? Surely if he loved and petted his dogs they would want to be near him and not have to be tied up near him. I assured him that guard dogs don't have to be taught to guard their owner and his property; if the dog loves you it is the most natural thing in the world for him to guard you.

I had no reply to my letter and as usual forgot what I thought was another ungrateful correspondent, but four months later I had one of the happiest possible letters from him enclosing some charming snaps of two of the dogs playing on the lawn with his wife, and two others sitting obediently in the background. His letter made me very happy, for it said the dogs were now completely different animals. He had taken my advice and given them much affection; he and his wife had taken them for walks, and trained them in obedience and above all played with them. Their suspicious natures had left them and he didn't think any thief or intruder would have a happy time. This man had the erroneous idea that you must not make a friend of a guard dog, that they must be more or less chained up, or left on their own, or they became soft and wouldn't do the job they were supposed to do. How wrong he was. Why, even the police dogs live at their handlers' homes and although they do not live in the house they are very much one of the family. And they are gentle creatures, not ferocious animals that in the interest of safety have to be kept away from human beings, unless tracking and catching criminals. Many people write to me to know, will I train their guard dog for them? Or where can they send him to be trained for such work? I assure them that they themselves must train the dog or he will guard the person who has trained him. Dogs are not machines that can be switched over at will and know whom they have to guard. It is far more difficult to untrain a guard dog than to train it. Any handler of such a dog will tell you that the biggest problem is to teach a dog to stop attacking on command rather than to teach it to do so.

People want to know what breed of dog is best for this job, and when I tell them my little miniature English Toy Terrier, weighing under ten pounds, is a dog I would be perfectly safe with, they think I am joking. It isn't always the biggest breed of dog that makes the best guard dog. Some of the small breeds, by their yapping alone would be adequate protection. Naturally, a big dog frightens an intruder, and few unwanted visitors would face a Great Dane, purely and simply because of its size and tremendous bark. There is no special breed to choose for guarding your property and person: there are fool dogs in all breeds who would happily go off with the burglar and never look back at their homes. But that comes from lack of training by the owner. When a dog has been the constant companion of the family and has received adequate obedience training, he instinctively guards and stays at home. As I have previously mentioned, the guarding instinct in some breeds can be a menace, and the dog becomes unsafe to take with you in public places. That is why I think an ordinary householder should not train his dog to be a guard dog: it takes an experienced handler to control a really trained guard dog, and an inexperienced handler will probably find himself in court, and his dog with an order to be kept under control. If the right attitude has been trained into your dog then he will guard.

The question of how to make a dog less friendly towards strangers is a difficult one, because, in general, people adore it when dogs run up to them and wag their tails and show pleasure at meeting them, when really they should give the dog a scolding and even possibly a quick slap and send him back to his owner. But one never gets the co-operation of the public. I find some of them a menace: if they see a trained dog standing outside a shop, they will not leave him alone, they allow their children to hug or pet him, in spite of the fact that the dog shows no interest, and gives them no welcome, and, what is worse, if you ask them to leave the dog in peace they are rude or say: 'Why shouldn't we pet dogs if we love them?' My reply to that is, 'If you were a real dog lover you wouldn't torture strange dogs with your unwanted attentions.' I point out to them that my trained dogs

It is not always the biggest breed that makes the best guard dog.

have interest in only one person, their mistress, and they only tolerate without biting the unwanted stroking because they are polite well-trained dogs.

Very often, these unwelcome attentions from the public will cause a nervous dog to get up and run away, and if he got killed or caused an accident those strangers would be responsible. But again, you must have the help of friends if you wish to train your dogs not to welcome strangers. You must ask people to call at your house and when the dog rushes out to greet them, they must give him a harsh word, or a quick slap if he really persists in forcing his attentions on them, and send him off. I know it is a horrid thing to have to do with a friendly dog, but it is for the dog's own sake. Train your

dog thoroughly in the two commands "Down" and "Leave" and he will not annoy visitors. Teach him that the command "Talk" means that he should go up to strangers and allow himself to be petted, and then you will really have a nice well-behaved dog. Teaching a dog the command "Talk" simply means taking him up to people and asking them to caress and speak to him, whilst you are praising and reassuring him all the time. It is amazing how quickly they learn. Personally, I do not wish my dogs to be friendly with all and sundry. They tolerate politely all advances made to them, and on the command "Talk" will politely wag their tails, but that is as far as it goes. They are my dogs and mine alone.

Chapter Nine

INDULGENCIES

To what extent does food govern a dog's mind? This is a question that most owners have had to face up to at one time or another, and many of them have told me they think food occupies most of the waking and thinking hours of their dogs. But I am quite sure that the people who own such dogs are very unlucky. The hunting instinct is extremely strong in most dogs; therefore, with problem dogs that chase and kill chickens or other livestock, the act is only what nature taught them to do many thousands of years ago. Their noses were designed for the act of tracking down and killing and, although domesticity has vastly reduced the number of breeds who hunt to kill, Greyhounds, Foxhounds and like breeds still, in fact, have this instinct highly developed. Many other breeds would hardly know what to do with the prey they had killed as they no longer suffer from hunger and, without this urge to spur them on, the kill is not vital.

In the wild state dogs killed twice or three times a week and ate until they nearly burst, after which they were quite happy to laze between orgies.

Nowadays from an early age our dogs' gastric juices have been trained to flow at fixed times each day and the desire to eat only becomes apparent normally at these times. It is true there are greedy dogs who will eat at all times of the day and night to the detriment of their figures and health, but these are the dogs that are easily trained by bribes. The dogs that are the most difficult to bribe are the naughtiest ones, because their minds are usually fixed on fighting another dog or running off into the distance, and I doubt if they think food will come from these escapades. The dogs who are most interested in food are the spoilt Poodles and Toy Dogs whose adoring owners give them snacks at all times. 'Just a leetle bitsie for Mitzie' has been known to do devastating things to Mitzie's mind and body. But here I blame the owner more than the dog.

Thieving is a natural instinct in all dogs. From the earliest days in the nest he has had to fight for his existence. In the days of the wild pack his ancestors hunted and stole from those other animals not clever enough to guard their prey. The instinct to steal is strong in the dog. The dog's mind is cunning in stealing and hiding for future use either food or some article he fancies. Much of it in the domestic dog today is done purely out of boredom. I have never known a well-trained dog, whose day is fully mapped out for it, steal. But the busy housewife, who owns a dog purely for the children to play with, often gets a thief as a result of lack of deep affection for anyone in particular by the dog, and from being bored with no work to do. All dogs should have work to do, whether it be only tricks to learn from the children or obedience exercises or some real work like gun work, etc. Without this, their brains are wasted, their minds pretty empty and their cunning increases. Watch how a thief dog sleeps almost with one eye open to deceive his owner into thinking he is fast asleep when what he is really waiting for is the opportunity to slip into the chickens' yard and steal their food, or into the owner's kitchen to see 'what's cooking' and to take whatever has been carelessly left about. The obvious fear on the dog's part when caught makes us realise dogs do know the difference between right and wrong if caught in the act, or even if heading for where the act is to take place. Obviously, to know they are doing wrong, they must at sometime or other have been scolded or punished for this self-same act.

Dogs are not born knowing what or what not to do, they only learn like children. Having once been punished, dogs remember, but like children they hope they won't be caught in the act. Dogs can be so conscience-stricken that I have seen an innocent one creep and crawl away in shame when another dog has committed a crime, and the innocent dog has been punished in error. I always remember as small children we had a big and a little dog. The big one had her puppies in the barn and rushed out when a tramp came too near, bit him, and streaked back before the tramp knew which dog had bitten him; the tiny one just stood there and watched. The tramp swore black and blue it was the little dog that had done the deed, and if I had not seen the other one do it, the little one would have been punished.

Sometimes dogs steal for praise worthy motives. Argus, my German Shepherd, made a nest and when Andy, his mate, had her puppies Argus, never having stolen before, went through a phase of thieving. One day I saw him steal some meat off the kitchen table and streak out to the orchard and drop it at the hole of the family and bark. I never scolded him, for I knew in this case, nature and the instinct to provide for his family was above all the training he had received. I think, therefore, owners should try to find the reason for the theft before correcting the dog. Sometimes worms produce a terrible hunger in dogs and a depraved appetite. When cured of these the dog no longer steals. Only punish when you are sure you as owner have not neglected your dog.

The teaching of food refusal in obedience tests was a very useful lesson to most dogs as people in shops often offer one's dog a titbit; when the dog turned his head away and refused to take it, it taught the shop-keeper not to repeat the offer. But it also had a disastrous effect on dogs sent to boarding kennels, as many refused to take food from the strange person who fed them and in one known case the dog nearly died. So now this test has been omitted from the schedule. The diet of some dogs needs to be rigidly controlled. These include dogs that have been castrated, old dogs whose figures have already exceeded normal girth, and greedy dogs who would never be satisfied with the small amounts given to them and would therefore get more cunning in the hope of getting more food. Nervous dogs wouldn't take the food or, if they did take it, would probably be sick almost immediately because the nerves have an adverse effect on digestion; and to feed a dog suffering from nervous exhaustion does more harm than good. That is why I never allow the dogs to be fed during a day's training. I always tell the owners to wait an hour after training ceases and then give the dog one big meal and let him rest.

I am sure the most important thing about food in connection with the dog is to give a properly balanced diet with sufficient vitamins and iron, etc; for a dog to be intelligent it has to be sufficiently and adequately nourished. If a dog is lacking minerals it will eat rubbish and especially dung. How can one expect to train a dog to be a nice companion in the house if he forever rolls in nasty things, eats manure and has a depraved appetite? Again no mind-reader can fathom the depths of a dog's mind and find the answer to his apparently depraved nature. Only common sense and knowledge of the dietetic needs of a dog learnt from experience, books or your vet will help you. The question of indulgences needs

much thought both from the point of view of the dog and that of the owner. I think more in the case of the latter. For is there one of us who at sometime or other in our lives cannot plead guilty to having indulged our dog? The mind of the dog tunes in very willingly to enjoy as many indulgences as he can persuade his owner to offer. His brain is never slow to take advantage of every kink in the defence armour of his owner. The eyes of a dog, the expression of a dog, the warmly wagging tail of a dog and gloriously cold damp nose of a dog were in my opinion all God-given for one purpose only, to make complete fools of us human beings.

I write reams about over-sentimental dog owners spoiling their dogs, yet know in my inner heart that not to do so takes supreme will power. For dogs are champions at heart-stealing. Even the wickedest dog in my school, who has severely bitten me, makes me long to hug him close to me and force out his evil wickedness, and I love him. Dogs are not slow-witted. They know when to push the slightest advantage they gain over their owner. How many dogs do we know who have committed some sin and who have cleverly evaded punishment by bringing mistress something to play with and, with an innocent look of deep trust, waited for her to join in the game when at that very moment she should be stick-in-hand, flaying the life out of him? But then that is the fascination of dogs. Why do hundreds of us give up our holidays to stay with them, cry our eyes out when we lose them, defend them against all those horrid people who don't love them and on our death beds make provision for them in preference to our needy families? It is because there is something about a dog that gets to you. Even if you own a problem one with all the evil the devil himself invented, you still know that, inside that dog, there is something very lovable – a dog that will never criticise you, a dog that doesn't care whether you are from the top or bottom drawer, who doesn't care whether you are clever or stupid, beautiful or hideous, rich or poor. He is yours and you are his.

At my residential training school in the past I am sure I have shocked pupils by feeding my dogs at meals. The dogs didn't ask, they just lay down waiting hopefully. My contention is, if my dogs don't annoy me and if I want to feed them, who is to say it is wrong? That is how I look upon all indulgences. If you like your dogs to sleep on your bed, putting up with the discomfort of not being able to turn over easily (especially if yours is a Great Dane) having a snoring bed companion, risking the hairs and dirt on the blankets and sheets, well, that is your business. What is my business, as a trainer, is to see these things don't happen if you wish otherwise. This is where a dog needs firm training, for a multitude of dogs get on their owner's beds and refuse to get off without a struggle and often bite the owner in the process. This is where a psychiatrist would easily be able to help, for he would know that, in the past, the dog had got away with it, and it needs no probing of the mind to know the dog much prefers a lovely warm bed with a warm owner in it, possibly a hot-water bottle, and certainly an eiderdown, to his own meagre offering of a basket and a blanket.

There is no doubt at all that dogs love luxury. 'Liver' instead of 'lights', beds instead of baskets, kisses instead of kicks and, if the owner doesn't want to bestow any of these luxuries on the dog, then the struggle to deny them to the dog must begin the moment the dog enters the house and must be carried on to his dying day. My own dog, star of thirty-seven films, winner of sixty-seven obedience prizes, herself defeated rigid obedience at the ripe old age of ten and a half years. Never in her life had she been allowed to lie in front of the fire. The heat is not good for dogs. She was too big and took up too much room. Her digestion was not so good that Camay was her only scent. Nevertheless, when we moved house she felt she would like a change and with audacious abandon lay full length in front of the fire. At first we laughed. Then I said her name in a shocked voice. She smiled a sickly smile and the tip of her tail wagged, uncertainty backed by hope and then, sensing my sympathy for her aging self, downed her head and feigned sleep. I pulled myself together and one word, "Sofa!" was enough to have her leap to her feet and climb on her own extremely comfortable sofa. You see her mind had picked up by telepathy that I didn't really mind her in front of the fire. In fact, I thought she looked rather beautiful with her brindled body outstretched. My own mind was weak. The dog knew at once. You cannot train a dog if you are weak or over-sentimental. They know and you are lost.

Are indulgences wrong for dogs? I think, under certain circumstances, no. What does count is, can you give up indulging the dog without fights or disagreeable behaviour the very

To what extent does food govern dog's mind?

moment you wish? If you can't, don't indulge your dog until you have trained him sufficiently well to be able to do what you wish at any time. The day the dog takes over you are lost. I do think one indulgence is very wrong, that is when you cannot leave your dog alone without his screaming or barking; should anything vital happen so that you could not stay with him, the neighbours would have to suffer appalling noise and you and the dog would be utterly miserable. I think dogs should always go with their owners whenever and wherever possible. Yet some places you go to don't admit dogs. Occasionally you are ill and may have to go to hospital or to a clinic. The dog can't go with you; he must stay at home or in your car. If neither of these things have been taught by previous training and endless tests, you won't know what to do. This sort of situation is bad. All dogs should be taught to stay quietly at home for some hours; as long as their routine is not broken too violently and they have been fed and exercised, there should be no hardship in staying at home for a dog.

We know titbits are bad for dogs; we

know sleeping in owner's beds is inclined to overheat them and make them delicate; we know above all that giving a command and then not having it carried out is fatal to a happy relationship. We know over-indulgent owners get spoilt dogs, who are a joy to none and a nuisance to all. I suggest we have a happy medium. Let's spoil our dogs sometimes, then we shall all be happy. The happiest people in this world are those who are for ever giving and making others happy. I am sure our dogs are included in that.

Chapter Ten

COMMON MISTAKES

Some owners are over-sentimental. Love is one thing, sentimentality to excess is another. Some dogs yelp when corrected when not in any way hurt. I proved this to one dog owner by kissing her dog which yelped in exactly the same way as he did when corrected; I didn't think my kiss was that lethal! Dogs like firm commands and loving praise when they do right. Owners use unkind thin-linked choke chains and jerk them upwards instead of downwards to correct the dog, and forget to take the left hand off the lead immediately after the jerk to allow the choke chain to release itself. They also jerk the lead with the palm of the hand facing upwards instead of downwards; this closes the choke chain on the dog's neck, and this may spoil the hair and is not kind in my opinion. Choke chains of my pattern should never close on the neck. Owners forget to say "what a good dog" when praising. The word 'what' has a magical effect on the dog and usually produces an instant happy rapport and obedience.

Owners' signals are ineffective or muddling; they give them bending forward so that the signal could be missed by the dog. Signals should be given firmly from the shoulder when standing upright. The hand giving the signal should be held away from the body so the dog can see the signal clearly. Owners often 'string up' show dogs on nylon leads; this must hurt the dog as nylon leads have sharp edges. Dogs should be trained to stand and look alert on the command "talk" which in my school means allow the judge to handle the dog, without the dog moving. If a dog can't hold his head up naturally, in my opinion he is not worth an award.

Owners fail to realise that with firm, confident, kind jerks and a happy tone of voice most dogs can be cured of nerves in a few hours. Never sympathise with a nervous dog. Jerk him on gaily, speaking to him in a happy voice, using my thick-linked choke chain, and above all, have a four foot lead held loosely over the two middle fingers of the right hand. Never close the right hand on the lead. A tight lead makes a dog nervous and dependant on his owner's support. When showing a dog, stand at least eighteen inches away from him to give him confidence on being handled by a judge. Owners should move fast when running a nervous dog; his tail then has to come up to balance him, and the habit grows and a natural tail carriage is established.

Owners fail when wishing a dog to be friendly, or be examined by a judge, to give the command "go and talk", at the same time pointing at the person the dog has to acknowledge or be handled by. Without this training the nervous dog may be suspicious of anyone approaching him and back away. This especially applies to judges in the show ring, who may be wary of approaching a dog who doesn't appear too friendly. The dog must be taught to stand still on the command "stand" and look up, wagging his tail if possible, at whoever is pointed at by the handler when given this 'talk' command. Owners have far too little range of voice tones. One needs low tones for commands given in a clear firm voice. Higher exuberant tones for praise when the dog has done well. A hard 'no nonsense' tone for wrong doing with deliberate disobedience.

Owners may still believe that a bitch's temperament is improved by having puppies; this is not so, she just passes on to her puppies bad temperament. They may also believe that to mate an over-sexed dog makes him better; this is also a fallacy, it makes his behaviour much worse, and he may even become bad tempered with other dogs into the bargain. Owners often don't realise that male and female human beings each have a different scent to a dog's nose, so that one often hears that dogs won't let men handle them. This may easily be true, as dogs know men from women by this different scent. A normal dog either likes or dislikes both men and women as a whole race, not one sex of human being. Individual men and women are attractive to dogs – why we just don't know. I have often noticed that people who profess to be great dog lovers may not be liked by dogs, curious though it may be. I feel this is because they rush in too fast, before the dog has time to sum them up. The holding out of one hand for the dog to smell in my opinion is the worst possible way to approach a dog, it shows the dog you do not feel confident that he will like you. I always approach a dog from the side if he is nervous, and stand beside him. Then I take the lead and make him walk with me.

Dog owners often think that dog experts can solve their problems over the phone where temperament faults exist in the dog. This is rarely so, the owner has to be met and summed up. They also hope if they send their dog away to be trained, he will return and obey them; in my opinion this is utterly wrong, for it is the owner who needs the training much more than the dog. In the greater number of cases, a sensible attitude towards a dog's mind, not assuming it to be equal to that of a human being, is all that is necessary to insure that he will be throughout his life man's best friend, a joy to all and a nuisance to no one.

APPENDIX

A range of other books, tapes and accessories are available to help you derive the full benefit from the Barbara Woodhouse approach to dog training.

Other titles in this series are:

Barbara Woodhouse On How Your Dog Thinks

Barbara looks at the world from the dog's viewpoint, and comes up with some new and surprising theories on dog behaviour. She shows owners how to understand their dogs and to communicate with them, not just by words and commands, but by tone of voice, and body language. In this book Barbara Woodhouse uses her rare gifts to break down the barriers, and helps all owners to achieve perfect companionship with their dogs.

Barbara Woodhouse On How To Train Your Puppy

IBarbara gives invaluable advice on house training, diet, exercise, and early training, and perhaps most important of all, she helps new owners get off to the right start, so that they can achieve a happy working relationship with their dog.

Barbara Woodhouse On Handling A Problem Dog

Whether it is an aggressive dog, a nervous dog, a roaming dog or a thief, Barbara Woodhouse believes that with proper understanding, most faults can be cured quickly and a happy relationship can be built up between owner and dog. At this time, more than any other, it is essential that all dogs are well behaved and live in harmony with their owners and with society. Barbara, who has trained some 19,000 dogs, tackles a wide spectrum of 'problem dogs' and comes up with sound, commonsense solutions.

Barbara Woodhouse On Keeping Your Dog Healthy

In a lifetime spent boarding, breeding and training dogs, she has come across all the most common conditions and complaints affecting dogs, and she gives practical, no-nonsense advice on all aspects of dog care, from diet, exercise and grooming to breeding, diagnosing health problems and nursing a dog through a serious illness. When you buy a dog, you are responsible for all its physical and mental needs, and this book tells you all you need to know to be a firm, fair and loving owner.

All these titles should be available through your local pet or book shop, price £3.99 each. In cases of difficulty they can be ordered direct from the publisher.
(Please add 75p per title towards P&P).
See address at the end of this section.

The Complete Woodhouse Guide To Dog Training

This is the definitive volume on dog training from Britain's best-loved expert.
Everything you need to know about the care and control of your dog; how to
understand his behaviour and how to get the best from him.
This book contains the very best of Barbara Woodhouse's writing
on a subject she understands like no other.
Available from good bookshops everywhere, price £14.95

*In case of difficulty The Complete Woodhouse Guide To Dog Training
can be ordered direct from the publisher.*
(Please add £1.50 towards P&P).
See address at the end of this section.

61

And if you've read the book, it is time to see the movie!

THE <u>WOODHOUSE</u> VIDEO
Barbara Woodhouse:
Quick Dog Training

A complete programme of obedience exercises for you and your dog.
This 90 minute video takes you step-by-step through all the essential
commands: Sit, Stay, Wait, Down, Leave and Recall.
PLUS house training, giving medicine, obedience in the car and on
the street, walking to heel and much, much more from the most
celebrated dog trainer in the world.

Price: £14.99
(plus £1.50 P&P)

Available ONLY from the publisher.
See address at the end of this section

BARBARA WOODHOUSE
CHOKE CHAINS AND LEADS

Are also available through the publisher

CHOKE CHAINS

Sizes at two–inch intervals
Twelve inches to eighteen inches £3.00
Twenty inches to Twenty-eight inches £3.50

To obtain the correct choke chain, measure over the top of the dog's
head, down over the ears and under the chin, then add two inches
and round up or down to the nearest size.
Please add 95p P&P to each order

LEADS

Approx four foot long in best quality bridle leather
Large or small trigger hooks £5.95
Please add 95p P&P to each order

BARBARA WOODHOUSE AUDIO CASSETTE

BASED ON THE SERIES
TRAINING DOGS THE WOODHOUSE WAY
Price: £5.95
(including postage and packing)

HOW TO ORDER

All the items described here can be ordered
direct from the publisher

RINGPRESS BOOKS LTD.,
SPIRELLA HOUSE, BRIDGE ROAD,
LETCHWORTH, HERTS SG6 4ET

Please remember to add postage and packing charge where
necessary and allow 21 days for delivery.

ACCESS and VISA card holder may order by telephone on
0462 674177

Office open 9am to 5pm Monday to Friday